Winston Grammar Program
Review Test

Sentence I: The old chair in the corner isn't very comfortable.

1. Name the two adverbs in Sentence I. ______________

   ____

2. Copy the prepositional phrase in Sentence I. ______________
3. What word does the prepositional phrase modify? ______________
4. Name the subject in Sentence I ______________
5. Name the contraction in Sentence I ______________

Sentence II: Take the coins to the bank please, Bob.

6. What is the subject in Sentence II? ______________
7. What is the direct object in Sentence II? ______________
8. What part of speech is *please*? ______________
9. What word is modified by *to the bank*? ______________
10. Name the noun of direct address in Sentence II ______________

Sentence III: She and I have brought Bob a huge gift.

11. Name the helping verb in Sentence III. ______________
12. Name the indirect object in Sentence III. ______________
13. How many personal pronouns are in Sentence III? ______________
14. Name the coordinating conjunction in Sentence III. ______________
15. What part of speech is *huge*? ______________

Sentence IV: Sal is an excellent student, but I am not.

16. Name two linking verbs in Sentence IV. ____________________

____

17. How many subjects are in Sentence IV? ____________________

18. Name the predicate nominative in Sentence IV. ____________________

19. Name the adjective in Sentence IV. ____________________

20. Name the article in Sentence IV. ____________________

Sentence V: Mr. Porter, the new principal, went to Yale.

21. Copy the prepositional phrase in Sentence V. ____________________

22. What word does this prepositional phrase modify? ____________________

23. Name the subject in Sentence V. ____________________

24. Name the appositive in Sentence V. ____________________

25. How many proper nouns are in Sentence V? ____________________

Sentence VI: Golly, we gave Tom the book yesterday; he hasn't returned it yet!

26. Name the indirect object in Sentence VI. ____________________

27. What part of speech is *yet*? ____________________

28. What word does *yet* modify? ____________________

29. Name the interjection in Sentence VI. ____________________

30. How many direct objects are in Sentence VI? ____________________

WORKSHEET 31

Identify only the parts of speech indicated for each group of sentences.
Sentences 1-5. Put a check (√) over all articles, and underline all nouns.
*tricky sentences

1. Mary and I saw Elvis Presley in a movie at the Argosy Theater on Wednesday.

2. The Oklahoma Sooners will play in the Orange Bowl on New Year's Eve.

*3. We came home Friday, but she wasn't there.

*4. European women enjoy American magazines.

5. We caught trout, bass and sunfish from the pier at the lake.

Sentences 6-10. Write **pron.** over all personal pronouns.

6. We will visit them before the Christmas vacation.

7. She gave it to them after she finished it.

8. They will tell us about it.

*9. Tell us a story and tuck us in.

*10. Thank you, Ned for the wonderful time we had.

WORKSHEET 32

Double underline all verbs and helping verbs in sentences 1-10. Circle **A** if the main verb is an action verb. Circle **L** if the main verb is a linking verb.
*tricky sentences

1. The diner closes at 10:00 p.m., Don. A L

2. Is the spider deadly or harmless? A L

3. Will you run around the block? A L

4. Have you spent the money yet? A L

5. He will become wealthy in a few years. A L

6. Sit and think about it for a while. 1. A L
2. A L

*7. She's afraid of the dark, Todd. A L

*8. The radio won't be fixed before tonight. A L

9. Chickens and turkeys can't fly away from the farm. A L

10. He'll be back from the Army in mid-February. A L

WORKSHEET 33

Write **adj.** over all adjectives, and write **adv.** over all adverbs. Draw arrows to the words they modify. Do not identify prepositional phrases.
*tricky sentences

1. The ugly monster attacked the beautiful princess.

2. He carefully turned the knob on the old safe.

*3. Doesn't Ted seem taller in the recent picture?

4. Dry weather always worries farmers.

*5. The birthday cake was very quickly eaten.

6. We camped Wednesday near the ghost town.

7. Soon you'll see the reason for the big decision.

*8. Up went the red and white balloon.

9. I am not very good with the yo-yo.

10. He rarely dines alone; he invites a neighbor or friend along.

WORKSHEET 34

Write **prep.** over all prepositions. Write **O.P.** over all objects of prepositions. Put all prepositional phrases in parentheses **( )**. Identify each phrase as an **ADJ.** or **ADV.** Draw an arrow to the word each phrase modifies.
*tricky sentences

1. I put the bucket in the shed.

2. We found the lost child near the highway.

3. The people in the parade waved at the crowd.

*4. Under the laws of nature, things don't fall up!

*5. We are tired of bacon and eggs.

6. Get under the umbrella, or you'll catch a cold.

7. We hid behind a bush until 11:30.

8. During recess, he fell on the playground.

9. The car sped around the curve on two wheels.

10. Throw the trash from the picnic into the can.

WORKSHEET 35

Underline all nouns, double-underline all verbs, and write **c.c.** over all coordinating conjunctions in sentences 1-5.
*tricky sentences

1. We were hungry yet happy after the hike.

2. Bill and I will build and furnish the new cabin.

3. You rake the leaves, and I will bag them.

*4. Never approach an angry dog; you may be sorry.

5. I've never cheated in school, nor will I!

Underline all nouns, double-underline all verbs, and put an exclamation mark over all interjections in sentences 6-10.

6. Wow, did you see the fireworks?

*7. Help! We can't find the way out.

8. Get out of here, mister!

9. Oh, you don't mean it!

10. Hey! I never knew you had a brother.

WORKSHEET 36

Underline every noun in the following sentences. Write **pron.** over every personal pronoun. Using the noun function cards 1-8, mark the function for each noun and each pronoun.

EVERY NOUN AND EVERY PRONOUN IN A SENTENCE MUST PERFORM A NOUN FUNCTION!

*tricky sentences

1. The sleek train raced across the plains toward the coast.

2. During a storm, the dog hides under the porch.

3. Tammy and I took the old car in the garage.

*4. We offered the nurse, Miss Edwards, a ride to the office.

*5. Tom, will you give Harry the message?

6. Uncle Sid and Father are brothers.

7. An apple pie contains one or two cups of sugar.

*8. Don't whistle in an elevator; it's bad luck!

9. Damon, the new boy on the block, showed me a picture of Hawaii.

10. David, Mr. Thompkins will be here soon; set the table.

WORKSHEET 37

Underline all nouns. Write **pron.** over every personal pronoun. Using the noun function cards, mark the function for each noun and each pronoun.

EVERY NOUN AND EVERY PRONOUN IN A SENTENCE MUST PERFORM A NOUN FUNCTION!

*tricky sentences

1. Barbers in most cities take Mondays off.

2. He and I studied for a test together.

3. Harvey, the bus driver, retired and moved to Texas.

4. Can you see the smoke from the campfire?

5. Please take the money from me and give it to them.

6. Helen picked us up after the debate.

7. It certainly is a clear and pleasant day, Dorothy.

*8. After college, he will become a wealthy man.

*9. I can't eat sweets, but she can; it's not fair!

10. Haven't you cleared the table yet, Sue?

WORKSHEET 38

Underline all nouns. Write **pron.** over every personal pronoun. Using the noun function cards, mark the function for each noun and each pronoun.

EVERY NOUN AND EVERY PRONOUN IN A SENTENCE MUST PERFORM A NOUN FUNCTION!

*tricky sentences

1. Admiral Foster was a hero during World War II.

2. Is math difficult for you, Mike?

3. It is illegal; you could go to jail!

4. Give them directions to the cabin.

*5. Chicago, a lovely place during the summer, is quite cold during the winter.

*6. Hand me the nails and the glue, Sis.

7. Walter, Adam, Sam, and Peter were hurt during the game.

8. We have modern rockets and bombers.

9. She gave Tom an "A," but I failed the course.

10. Barbi and Nancy are twins.

WORKSHEET 39

Underline all nouns. Write **pron.** over every personal pronoun. Using the noun function cards, mark the function for each noun and each pronoun.

EVERY NOUN AND EVERY PRONOUN IN A SENTENCE MUST PERFORM A NOUN FUNCTION!

*tricky sentences

1. I hate spaghetti; do you have a second choice?

2. Colorado is a nice place for a vacation.

3. We built a tree house for the children.

4. The frost on the window sparkles.

5. Mr. Abbot, will you explain the crazy picture?

6. The movie at the drive-in, *Grease,* appeals to teenagers.

*7. The old farmer spent Saturday in town.

8. The loud noises from the factory give us a headache.

WORKSHEET 40

Underline all nouns. Write **pron.** over every personal pronoun. Using the noun function cards, mark the function for each noun and each pronoun.

EVERY NOUN AND EVERY PRONOUN IN A SENTENCE MUST PERFORM A NOUN FUNCTION!

*tricky sentences

1. Eric, did you use the scissors last?

2. He and I won't be actors in the play.

3. On winter nights we listen to the weather report.

*4. Give us ten minutes; we aren't finished yet.

5. Nashville, "Music City U.S.A.," has four new hotels.

6. Fix the pipes, or they will cause problems.

*7. We were ten-year-olds, but we understood.

8. The policeman handed me a ticket.

9. A bulb broke, but we replaced it quickly.

10. The dirty water is not fit for humans.

WORKSHEET 41

Worksheet 41 involves possessive adjectives. Your new orange card with the blue border lists these words. Mark all nouns and pronouns and indicate noun functions. Write **adj.** over all adjectives, and draw arrows to the words they modify. Use your cards. Do not identify prepositional phrases.
*tricky sentences

1. My major problem in math is long division.

2. He took our alarm clock to his room.

3. Your picture in the yearbook is fuzzy.

*4. Get your hands off my pizza!

5. Her engagement was announced at their party.

6. Our country wants peace in the world.

7. I forgot his name, but Mr. Roberts will probably remind me.

8. The clear and shiny stone in her ring is not a real diamond.

*9. My shoes are too big for him, and his shirt is too small for me.

10. Take my picture with our new camera, Tom.

WORKSHEET 42

You have been given a possessive pronoun card. Possessive pronouns always perform noun functions. Note that **his** is sometimes an adjective. Be careful when you see **his**. If it performs a noun function, it is a pronoun. Identify all nouns and pronouns; mark their functions.
*tricky sentences

1. She used mine; hers was broken.

2. Ours won't be ready until noon.

3. Mr. Chapman repeated the story for us.

*4. Do it now!

*5. It was his fault and not mine.

6. His can't be very expensive.

7. You kept mine, so I'll keep yours.

8. They found us quite lost in the traffic.

9. We located theirs, but yours are missing.

10. I wrote the book during my vacation.

WORKSHEET 43

Underline all nouns and mark all pronouns. Indicate the noun function each noun and pronoun performs. Mark all adjectives and draw arrows to the words they modify.

*tricky sentences

1. His was never found until our search.

2. My onion patch is doing very well.

3. Get your guns, Butch; we're in big trouble!

4. Yours is fresh, but ours is stale.

5. Her eyeglasses have frames similar to ours.

6. My dog is healthy, but his has fleas.

7. We watched *Oliver Twist* on your television.

8. The old miner finally found his big strike.

9. Our only chance for victory is lost!

*10. Give mine some gas, and we'll start it.

*11. We rested my horse, and we gave hers a bucket of water.

*12. The guilt is mine; I deserve a punishment.

WORKSHEET 44

This worksheet contains many possessives. Underline all nouns. Mark all pronouns with **pron.** Indicate all noun functions. Write **adj.** above adjectives and draw arrows to the words they modify.
*tricky sentences

1. We saw Peter's new suit.

2. The cow's stall was at the back of the barn.

* 3. Ted's is new; mine is quite old.

4. Give my favorite charity a donation.

5. They delivered Mr. Porter's mail to Mrs. Brown's house.

* 6. The team–members' major problem was cooperation.

7. The owner left his doors open over the weekend.

8. My papers are ready, but theirs are not.

9. The Yankees' chances are slim, but I'll root for them.

10. The Senators' vote was very close, but ours was not, Mr. President.

WORKSHEET 45

Underline all nouns. Write **pron.** over all pronouns. Indicate noun functions. Write **adj.** over all adjectives and draw a line to words modified. These are all tricky!

1. She gave mine an "A," but his rated an "A+!"

2. Dave's was last on the list; his last name starts with a "Z."

3. California's taxes are high, but Utah's are low.

*4. Of all the pictures on the wall, yours is best.

5. We went to see *Yours, Mine, and Ours*, a great movie.

6. The victory is ours; we deserve their applause.

7. It's yours, but I want a bite anyway.

8. We saw Frank's new car, and it's a beauty.

9. Hey, I never got mine; you must have taken it.

10. We sang *Mine Eyes Have Seen The Glory*.

11. The cows' barn is near the horses' shed.

12. Buy his; it's the best one.

WORKSHEET 46

The following words are often either adjectives or pronouns. **They are pronouns if they perform noun functions in a sentence.** They are adjectives if they modify nouns.

this	that	these	those	which
whose	what	all	any	another
anyone	both	each	either	everybody
nobody	none	one, two, three....		something
other	several	somebody	some	someone

In the sentences below, underline all nouns, write **pron.** over all pronouns, and mark all adjectives **adj.** Mark all nouns and pronouns for noun function. Draw arrows from adjectives to the words they modify.

1. Few people want their children in that school.

2. Several plants died in the sun, but some didn't.

3. Three of us will go with them.

4. Many foreign countries trade with the U.S.A.

5. I took two, and she took five.

6. Nobody came to the door of their apartment.

7. She gave most of her wealth to charity.

8. You may have either one, Tom.

WORKSHEET 47

Underline all nouns. Write **pron.** over all pronouns. Mark all noun functions. Identify adjectives with **adj.**, and draw arrows to the words they modify.
*tricky sentences

1. This is my favorite movie.

2. Which car won the race?

*3. Some laws don't seem fair to me.

4. Few of the questions were difficult.

5. Nobody came to the meeting from Colorado.

6. Both red trucks were driven safely.

7. Too few people go to that church.

*8. Find someone nice for our teacher, Mr. Block.

9. Nobody can tell me about this program tonight.

10. Each boy will learn his lesson from that accident.

WORKSHEET 48

Underline all nouns. Write **pron.** over all pronouns. Mark all noun functions. Identify adjectives with **adj.**, and draw arrows to the words they modify.
*tricky sentences

1. These wild rabbits ate all of the lettuce in the garden.

2. Anybody over 18 can drive a car in this state.

3. Most good restaurants are full of people on Saturdays.

4. She offered him both, but he took neither.

5. Don't drink any of that, Roger.

*6. I've been in Atlanta a few weeks.

7. The other chair might be more comfortable.

*8. Do many movie stars visit this hotel, sir?

9. All of our time is spent near the pool.

10. Two or three will be enough for the day.

WORKSHEET 49

Words ending in **–self** or **–selves** are pronouns. If they perform a noun function, indicate their use in the sentence. Mark all pronouns with **pron.** and indicate their functions (if any).

*tricky sentences

1. She made herself a cup of soup.

2. We watched ourselves on the evening news.

3. They made a home for themselves in the forest.

*4. I will conduct the meeting myself.

5. Get yourself a new umbrella.

*6. Be kind to yourself; get some rest.

7. I made a promise to myself over the weekend.

8. The dog bit itself on the tail.

*9. The President himself will appear on the broadcast.

*10. They did the more difficult work themselves.

WORKSHEET 50

Who, whom, which, what, whose often introduce questions. If they perform noun functions, they are pronouns. If they modify nouns, they are adjectives.
Identify all nouns and pronouns in the following sentences. Mark all noun functions.
ON A SEPARATE SHEET, REARRANGE QUESTIONS AS STATEMENTS IF NECESSARY.

Example: Who will be our teacher?

P.N.
pron.
Our teacher will be who?

*tricky sentences

1. Whose can we borrow today?

2. Which can move fastest?

*3. What decision have you reached?

4. What will the answer be, Ted?

5. Who will clean the den after the party?

6. Whom can I ask about the garage sale?

7. Which team will wear white jerseys?

*8. Whose paint spilled on the new carpet?

WORKSHEET 51

Mark all nouns, pronouns, and adjectives. Identify all noun functions. Rearrange questions as statements if necessary.
*tricky sentences

1. Which car will we take to the lake?

2. From whom can we expect the best papers?

3. What will happen after the first act?

4. Can we spend a few minutes on that?

5. Who should be named to the post?

6. Which part of the machine is most dangerous?

7. For whom is it more difficult?

8. We saw several; none were available.

*9. Who will be successful in the end?

10. What is your final answer, Fran?

WORKSHEET 52

The words **where, why, when**, and **how** often introduce simple questions. When they do, they are adverbs. Change questions to statements if necessary, and mark all adverbs, adjectives, nouns, and pronouns. Identify all noun functions. Draw arrows from adverbs and adjectives to the words they modify.
*tricky sentences

1. Why can't we go to the rally?

2. When will Tina be ready for her trip?

*3. Whose bike can we borrow for the race?

4. How did the policeman find the burglar?

5. When can we expect an answer, Mr. Blake?

*6. How often do hurricanes cause damage here?

*7. Why can't Peter give Tom his tickets?

8. Where will the tree fall?

9. How can you work on the roof in the dark?

10. What time is it in New York, Captain?

QUIZ -- Lessons 41-52

Identify all nouns and pronouns. Indicate noun functions. Label all adjectives and adverbs, and draw arrows to words modified.

1. Where are you, Fred?

2. What time is it in Chicago?

3. This is fine, but that won't do.

4. Help yourself to some of the candy.

5. When will the Mayor make his decision?

6. Where is mine?

7. Why doesn't he make himself a cup of coffee?

8. Who will clean the gym after the game tonight?

WORKSHEET 53

Identify all nouns, pronouns, verbs and adjectives. Draw arrows from adjectives to the words they modify. Mark all noun functions. Watch out for words ending in **-ing**.
*tricky sentences

1. Are you collecting pretty rocks?

* 2. The magician's tricks are really amazing.

* 3. The magician's tricks are amazing the children.

4. This is the cutting edge of the saw.

5. Why are you crying, Sis?

6. Who is calling me?

7. We will be traveling to the island by boat.

8. The falling rocks nearly hit the old shack.

9. A thrilling moment came near the end of the inning.

10. Who will be counting the ballots today?

WORKSHEET 54

Identify all nouns, pronouns, verbs and adjectives. Draw arrows from adjectives to the words they modify. Mark all noun functions. Watch out for words ending in **-ing**.
*tricky sentences

1. Will you be climbing the mountain today?

2. The meeting was very boring.

3. An interesting point was brought to my attention.

4. He is a trusting person: be kind to him.

5. We were only skating around for ten minutes.

6. Marge couldn't be waiting for him.

7. The flaming rocket disappeared into the evening sky.

8. Is he getting himself into trouble, officer?

9. The barking dog is coming too close to the baby!

--If you get #10 correct, pat yourself on the back!--

* 10. Darling, are you painting the ceiling in the morning?

WORKSHEET 55

Identify all nouns, pronouns, verbs and adjectives. Draw arrows from adjectives to the words they modify. Mark all noun functions. Watch out for words ending in **-ing**.
*tricky sentences

1. The weeds are growing too fast.

2. We will be needing more medicine, Doctor Jones.

*3. This can be confusing to some students.

4. Why are we keeping that stale bread?

5. He'll be following us in his sports car.

6. Our meeting place has been changed.

*7. Is this confusing you, Charles?

8. The old lawyer was defending his last client.

9. Wiggling worms catch more fish.

10. The cooking class is making a special dish.

WORKSHEET 56

Identify all nouns, pronouns, and adjectives; mark noun functions and draw arrows.
*tricky sentences

1. The tired horse had run a good race.

2. We have rescued the mistreated children.

3. Those will be packed with the others.

*4. Her dress was torn near the hem.

5. We were certainly excited about your wedding.

6. Will he be allowing himself the luxury of a cruise?

7. Where are the completed forms?

8. It has been suggested; why do you ask?

9. I have seen the scrubbed floors.

*10. The young athlete was flattered by the applause.

WORKSHEET 57

Mark all nouns, pronouns, verbs and adjectives. Identify all noun functions. Draw arrows to words modified.

1. We admired the beautiful climbing roses.

2. Who has forgotten the answer, Miss Perkins?

3. Driving school is required in many states.

4. Put the paid and stamped bills in a stack on my desk.

5. Someone has taken the sugar and creamer.

6. They carried the slain warrior back to the weeping widow.

7. The woven fabric is too expensive.

8. Our enemy has fled to the hills.

9. Chirping birds can be annoying.

10. Are they tearing the building down yet?

WORKSHEET 58

Mark all nouns, pronouns, and verbs in the following sentences. Identify all noun functions. Mark all conjunctions with **c.c.**

Coordinating Conjunctions: **and but for yet or nor ;**

Correlative Conjunctions:

both.....and | **not only....but also**
either...or | **neither......nor**

*tricky sentences

1. Either the rain will stop, or we'll cancel the picnic.

*2. Not only am I graduating, but I am also at the top of my class.

3. Either leave or start your work, Bill.

4. We received both a lecture and a punishment.

5. I want neither the salad nor the dessert.

6. The jungle cat is not only dangerous, but he is also smart.

*7. Both are trying, but neither will succeed.

8. Either I get my way, or I'll stop the game.

WORKSHEET 59

Mark all simple infinitives with parentheses. Indicate their parts of speech. If the infinitive is a noun, mark its function. If the infinitive is an adjective or adverb, draw an arrow from the infinitive to the word modified.
*tricky sentences

1. I don't like to brag.

2. My little dog is very eager to please.

3. Now that was a day to remember!

4. It was very unpleasant to experience.

*5. Go to the gym to exercise.

6. Wait for your directions to begin.

*7. To build, we will need a permit from the county.

8. I want to follow, but you are going too fast.

WORKSHEET 60

Mark all simple infinitives with parentheses. Indicate their parts of speech. If the infinitive is a noun, mark its function. If the infinitive is an adjective or adverb, draw an arrow from the infinitive to the word modified.
*tricky sentences

1. We certainly need to leave, Johnny.

2. Scouts returned to the fort to report.

3. The baby started to cry.

*4. To succeed, we must start a new business.

5. It is difficult to understand.

6. To remember, I tie a string on my finger.

7. Start to read; you only have another ten minutes.

*8. Get to bed and try to sleep.

WORKSHEET 61

Underline all nouns and write **pron.** above all pronouns. Identify all noun functions. Gerunds are verb forms ending in **-ing** which perform noun functions. Underline all gerunds and identify their noun functions.

Example: S P.N.

Stealing is a serious crime.
(Stealing is a gerund.)

*tricky sentences

1. We tried skating, but it was too difficult.

2. He went out for wrestling.

3. The dentist charges me $10 for a filling.

4. The old man smokes cigars after eating.

5. I could hear the singing.

6. Voting is a citizen's duty in America.

7. The children reached the bottom of the hill by sliding on snow saucers.

8. Before relaxing, the mowing should be done.

WORKSHEET 62

Underline all nouns and write **pron.** above all pronouns. Identify all noun functions. Underline all gerunds and identify their noun functions. Remember: Gerunds are verb forms ending in **-ing** which perform noun functions.

Example: S P.N.
Stealing is a serious crime.
(Stealing is a gerund.)

*tricky sentences

1. Fighting is not allowed on the playground.

2. We saw the shooting yesterday.

*3. I find cooking very difficult.

*4. Watching from the window, the old lady was amused by the giggling children.

5. Are you paying your bills on time, Barbara?

6. We got a light sprinkling of rain today.

7. Lying is forbidden in a court of law.

*8. Clam digging can be hard work.

9. Hunting dogs are often good house pets.

10. We drove in the country before returning.

QUIZ -- Lessons 41-62

Identify all nouns and pronouns. Mark noun functions. Label all adjectives and adverbs. Draw arrows to words modified. Watch out for participles, infinitives. and gerunds.

1. I like to sleep; please don't wake me.

2. Traveling in Mexico can be dangerous.

3. She attends sewing class on Wednesdays.

4. The battleship was destroyed in the harbor.

5. This will certainly be a game to remember.

6. Speeding can result in a trip to jail.

7. The torn page was glued to the cardboard.

8. Exhausted, we started to return.

WORKSHEET 63

Mark all subjects and verbs. Circle the number of subject-verb combinations to each sentence below.

Example: S
She likes chocolate. (1) 2 3

*tricky sentences

1. Bill will lock the door. 1 2 3

2. We have a problem. 1 2 3

3. We promised to be there. 1 2 3

4. Circles were drawn on the page. 1 2 3

5. Their plans and hopes were realized. 1 2 3

*6. Arguing will get you nowhere; give up. 1 2 3

7. She and I waited and rested. 1 2 3

8. Provide us with food, or we'll go away. 1 2 3

9. Set the clock for 6:00; I need to get up. 1 2 3

*10. She tried but failed to get her diploma. 1 2 3

WORKSHEET 64

Mark all subjects and verbs. Circle the number of subject-verb combinations to each sentence below.

Example: S S
Walter caught a cold, but Sara didn't. 1 (2) 3 4

*tricky sentences

1. Pick the beans near the fence first. 1 2 3 4

2. George, please sit behind the desk. 1 2 3 4

*3. We explored caves, climbed mountains,

and hiked trails. 1 2 3 4

4. Donald can't decide if he wants to go. 1 2 3 4

5. Going to town is a big event. 1 2 3 4

6. I want to see New York before I leave. 1 2 3 4

7. Fill the canteen, but don't drink any of the water. 1 2 3 4

8. You must be mad; that could be dangerous! 1 2 3 4

9. Jane made supper while Abe cleaned the den. 1 2 3 4

10. The dog barks; the cat howls; the birds chirp;

I can't get any peace! 1 2 3 4

WORKSHEET 65

Count subject-verb combinations in the following sentences, and put brackets **[ ]** around each clause.

Example: [When we win,] [we celebrate.] 1 ② 3

*tricky sentences

1. The robins chirped as we approached the nest. 1 2 3

2. The teacher took over while the principal was away. 1 2 3

3. Jim can't do the job because he is ill. 1 2 3

4. Until the votes were counted, we were nervous. 1 2 3

*5. Get the water while I set the table. 1 2 3

6. If the money arrives, we will be able to go. 1 2 3

7. Painting with these brushes is impossible. 1 2 3

8. The puppies and kittens don't get along. 1 2 3

WORKSHEET 66

Count subject-verb combinations in the following sentences, and put brackets **[ ]** around each clause.

Example: [When we <u>win</u>,] [we <u>celebrate</u>.] 1 ② 3

(S above "we" in both clauses)

*tricky sentences

1. I am not listening to you, Tom. 1 2 3

2. Although he attended college, he didn't find work. 1 2 3

3. Bill, wait until the rest of us finish. 1 2 3

4. Happy days followed their arrival in Paris. 1 2 3

5. May I talk with Sandy while you sleep? 1 2 3

6. Vacuum the rug before you make the bed. 1 2 3

7. I left because I was tired. 1 2 3

8. After the rain stopped, the game resumed. 1 2 3

*9. After showering, he read the paper by the pool. 1 2 3

10. Though I disagree, you may have a point. 1 2 3

WORKSHEET 67

In the following sentences, mark and count subject-verb combinations, bracket clauses, and mark dependent clauses. Draw arrows from clauses to the words they modify. Label subordinating conjunctions **S.C.**

Example: (S.C. over "Before"; S over "we" and "we"; ADV. with arrow to "pack")

[Before we <u>leave</u>,] [we <u>will</u> <u>pack</u> the car.] 1 ②3

1. The invaders were beaten back after the troops arrived. 1 2 3

2. While the boys were in town, we relaxed. 1 2 3

3. We woke up because the train came by. 1 2 3

4. Come back soon if you can. 1 2 3

5. Since it's yours, you may keep it. 1 2 3

*6. As I toured the museum, I was truly amazed. 1 2 3

7. We were eager, so we got up early. 1 2 3

8. She is taller than he is. 1 2 3

WORKSHEET 68

In the following sentences, mark and count subject-verb combinations, bracket clauses, and mark dependent clauses. Draw arrows from clauses to the words they modify. Label subordinating conjunctions.
*tricky sentences

1. Before we knew it, the play was over. 1 2 3

2. They aimed the water where smoke appeared. 1 2 3

3. She was late because she stopped for gas. 1 2 3

4. Do the homework before we leave for the movie. 1 2 3

5. It can be expensive if you own a plane. 1 2 3

6. We tried to return when the flood waters

   were too high. 1 2 3

7. After hours had gone by, we rose to leave. 1 2 3

*8. Watch, listen, and think because this may

   be a most important decision. 1 2 3

WORKSHEET 69

Count subject-verb combinations. Bracket all clauses. Identify subordinating conjunctions (S.C.) and draw arrows from adverb clauses to the words they modify.

Examples:

A. [The beach was fine,] but [the lake was rough.] 1 ② 3

ADV.

S.C.

B. [You try to read] [while we are waiting,]

or [you'll be wasting time.] 1 2 ③

*tricky sentences

1. As we reached the top of the hill, the

car stalled. 1 2 3

2. Bob and his brother run a store in Tucson. 1 2 3

3. We are planning to go, but we may not arrive

until the second half begins. 1 2 3

4. City workers struck when they didn't get

a raise. 1 2 3

5. He runs and bats well, but he can't catch

the ball. 1 2 3

*6. Although we have little money, we are happy. 1 2 3

WORKSHEET 70

Count subject-verb combinations. Bracket all clauses. Identify subordinating conjunctions (S.C.) and draw arrows from adverb clauses to the words they modify.

*tricky sentences

1. After you leave I'll give him a call. 1 2 3

2. She is planning every detail of the wedding. 1 2 3

3. Until new medicines are developed, cancer

   will be a dangerous threat. 1 2 3

*4. Run when you see a snake, or you may

   be sorry. 1 2 3

5. If we are correct, we'll be happy when

   we open this gift. 1 2 3

*6. Try to understand; it wasn't here when

   we arrived. 1 2 3

WORKSHEET 71

Put brackets around all clauses. Identify subordinating conjunctions. Draw arrows from adverb clauses to the words they modify. Remember that coordinating conjunctions which connect clauses are left <u>outside</u> the brackets.

*tricky sentences

*1. Simple problems can become large problems if

we worry more than we should. 1 2 3

2. We are happiest when we work and

when we succeed. 1 2 3

3. After a year in jail, he'll be jobless unless

we help him. 1 2 3

4. Until the holiday, please save your money so

we can shop. 1 2 3

5. Since you arrived, I've been happy because

you cheer me up. 1 2 3

6. Order more pencils before we run out ;

we need them. 1 2 3

QUIZ -- Lessons 41-71

Count subject-verb combinations in each sentence. Bracket all clauses. Identify subordinating conjunctions. Label adverb clauses and draw arrows to words modified.

1. I cried when she left. 1 2 3

2. Because we won, we advanced to the finals. 1 2 3

3. As the car slowed down, the driver waved at us. 1 2 3

*4. Before dinner, but after 4:00, please run the errands. 1 2 3

5. It was unpleasant when he entered the room. 1 2 3

6. Nobody claimed it, so I took it home. 1 2 3

*7. Why start smoking when you know the dangers? 1 2 3

8. If I can push and if you can help, we'll get there. 1 2 3

WORKSHEET 72

Count subject-verb combinations. Bracket all clauses. Identify adjective clauses. Mark relative pronouns (**R.P.**) and subordinating conjunctions (**S.C.**). Draw arrows to words modified.

ADJ.
R.P.
Example: [The one [that we chose] is over here.] 1 (2) 3

1. He is a fine man whom we admire greatly. 1 2 3

2. The paper which received a "B" deserved

   an "A." 1 2 3

3. The suntan that I had in July has faded. 1 2 3

4. She's the one who saved the child. 1 2 3

5. The boy who sang is my cousin. 1 2 3

6. A Republican whose party is behind him can win. 1 2 3

WORKSHEET 73

Count subject-verb combinations. Bracket all clauses. Identify adjective and adverb clauses. Mark relative pronouns **(R.P.)** and subordinating conjunctions **(S.C.)**. Draw arrows to words modified.
*tricky sentences

1. The ghost that he described must have been frightening. 1 2 3

2. The one which I chose was expensive. 1 2 3

3. A man whom we remember well is Mr. Bates. 1 2 3

4. An athlete who tries hard may qualify for the Olympics. 1 2 3

*5. A senator whom we respect and who cares for us will be elected. 1 2 3

6. When summer arrives, we enjoy the breezes that blow in from the sea. 1 2 3

WORKSHEET 74

Identify all clauses and mark them accordingly. Put **S.C.** above all subordinating conjunctions, and put **R.P.** above all relative pronouns. Watch out for relative pronouns which are not expressed. Put them in parentheses **( )**.

Example: (ADJ. — R.P. (that))

[The car [I bought] runs well .] 1 ② 3

*tricky sentences

1. The crime you committed is serious. 1 2 3

2. A problem which we recently discussed

   is solved. 1 2 3

3. Two ideas you had seem quite original. 1 2 3

4. Try someone whom you haven't seen lately. 1 2 3

*5. Because we were late, we lost the chance

   we had. 1 2 3

*6. Multiply the numbers before you get the

   answer you want. 1 2 3

7. The schools I visited seemed very disorganized. 1 2 3

WORKSHEET 75

Identify all clauses and mark them accordingly. Put **S.C.** above all subordinating conjunctions, and put **R.P.** above all relative pronouns. Watch out for relative pronouns which are not expressed. Put them in parentheses **( ).**
*tricky sentences

1. The woman we elected is doing a fine job. 1 2 3 4

2. The important letter, which didn't arrive until 11:00, contained new information. 1 2 3 4

*3. Go where you please, but remember the rules we agreed to follow. 1 2 3 4

4. The person you need to ask is not here. 1 2 3 4

5. Your uncle, whom we truly admired, will be missed. 1 2 3 4

6. Pick the ones you want from the pile near the door. 1 2 3 4

QUIZ -- Lessons 41-75

Bracket all clauses. Label dependent clauses **ADJ.** or **ADV.**. Draw arrows to words modified. Label subordinating conjunctions **S.C.** and relative pronouns **R.P.**.

1. That's the man who gave me the money. 1 2 3

2. Because our plane was late, we missed the meeting. 1 2 3

3. The governor is a man whom we respect. 1 2 3

4. The courses I took were difficult. 1 2 3

5. The radio that you ordered has come in. 1 2 3

6. The restaurant on the side of the road near the beach closed for the holiday. 1 2 3

WORKSHEET 76

<u>Bracket only dependent clauses</u>. Label adverb and adjective clauses; identify words modified by drawing arrows. Label relative pronouns and subordinating conjunctions. Draw a circle around each noun clause or noun which acts as a direct object.
*tricky sentences

1. I know what she said. 1 2 3

2. We have learned how it happened. 1 2 3

3. The one I selected was green. 1 2 3

* 4. Give whatever help you can to the cause. 1 2 3

5. Sally deserved whatever she got. 1 2 3

6. You may invite whomever you wish. 1 2 3

WORKSHEET 77

Bracket only dependent clauses. Label adverb and adjective clauses; identify words modified by drawing arrows. Label relative pronouns and subordinating conjunctions. Draw a circle around each noun clause which acts as a direct object.
*tricky sentences

1. Put the jacket that got wet in the dryer. 1 2 3

2. The police asked why she did it. 1 2 3

3. I don't remember which boy did it. 1 2 3

4. We tried what seemed most logical. 1 2 3

5. I realized who it was. 1 2 3

* 6. Don't tell me how the movie ends. 1 2 3

WORKSHEET 78

Bracket dependent clauses. Label and draw arrows for adjective and adverb clauses. Noun clauses should be marked for function: circle direct objects, box indirect objects. Mark subordinating conjunctions and relative pronouns.
*tricky sentences

1. Whenever we go on a picnic, we see ants. 1 2 3

2. I gave the man who rang the bell one dollar. 1 2 3

*3. I wish whoever wins the very best luck. 1 2 3

4. Do whatever you wish; I don't care. 1 2 3

5. The new fence, which cost us one thousand dollars, isn't very sturdy. 1 2 3

6. The teacher gave whoever came late a detention. 1 2 3

7. The ideas he has were quite unusual. 1 2 3

8. He determined who was arriving before he opened the door. 1 2 3

WORKSHEET 79

Bracket all dependent clauses and label them. Noun clauses include direct objects, indirect objects, and <u>predicate nominatives</u>. Label relative pronouns **R.P.** and subordinating conjunctions **S.C.**

*tricky sentences

1. He does whatever he wishes. 1 2 3

2. The special guest can be whomever you wish. 1 2 3

3. This house will never be what I prefer, Jim. 1 2 3

4. They did what we predicted. 1 2 3

5. Refuse whoever asks a free ticket. 1 2 3

*6. Is this what you expected? 1 2 3

*7. Whenever I give whoever fails a low grade,

he complains. 1 2 3

*8. He became what he wished, a fireman. 1 2 3

QUIZ -- Lessons 41-79

Bracket all dependent clauses and identify their parts of speech. Label relative pronouns and subordinating conjunctions. Label noun functions of clauses.

1. If I can't have whatever I want, I'm leaving. 1 2 3

2. I found what you lost. 1 2 3

3. I think you may fail, but you should try anyway. 1 2 3

4. Extend whoever loses a friendly handshake. 1 2 3

5. This is not what I ordered, sir. 1 2 3

6. Believe what you wish, but I didn't do

   what you say I did. 4 5 6

WORKSHEET 80

Bracket and label all dependent clauses and relative pronouns. These sentences include noun clauses functioning as objects of prepositions.
*tricky sentences

1. Sit with whomever you please. 1 2 3

2. From what I understand, he is very ill. 1 2 3

*3. Under what conditions will you agree? 1 2 3

*4. Whatever do you mean, Mr. Porter? 1 2 3

5. The teacher looked over what I wrote. 1 2 3

6. I am afraid of what may happen. 1 2 3

7. I can't see what the problem is. 1 2 3

8. Is she disturbed by what you said? 1 2 3

WORKSHEET 81

Bracket and label all dependent clauses, relative pronouns, and subordinating conjunctions. These sentences may include noun clauses functioning as appositives.
*tricky sentences

1. The final answer, whatever it may be, will be found in this report. 1 2 3

2. They will spy on whoever threatens them. 1 2 3

3. Your roommate, whomever you choose, must be a junior or a senior. 1 2 3

4. Try a piece of whatever she bakes ; it will be delicious. 1 2 3

5. Can I be seated where you are? 1 2 3

*6. A man who saves will be happy when he retires. 1 2 3

7. This jacket, what I wanted for Christmas, pleases me. 1 2 3

8. We will agree to whatever you suggest. 1 2 3

WORKSHEET 82

Bracket and label all dependent clauses, relative pronouns, and subordinating conjunctions. These sentences may include noun clauses functioning as subjects.
*tricky sentences

1. What is easily found may not be valuable. 1 2 3

2. Whoever is guilty will be severely punished. 1 2 3

*3. That boy will do whatever we ask. 1 2 3

4. Whatever you decide will be remembered for years. 1 2 3

5. The good chance we had is gone. 1 2 3

6. Write down what we say, Tom. 1 2 3

*7. Give what you can to the church where you

worship. 1 2 3

8. They were amazed at what they saw. 1 2 3

WORKSHEET 83

Label and bracket all dependent clauses, relative pronouns and subordinating conjunctions.
*tricky sentences

1. We'll never understand how you can sleep
   when there is so much noise. 1 2 3

*2. Say what you will; I still disagree with you. 1 2 3

3. Wherever you go, he follows. 1 2 3

4. I know what you are doing. 1 2 3

5. Stand up for what you believe. 1 2 3

6. My check, what I came for in the first place,
   hasn't been written. 1 2 3

*7. You are the person I admire most. 1 2 3

8. Take whatever catches your eye before the
   other shoppers arrive. 1 2 3

WORKSHEET 84

Label and bracket all dependent clauses, relative pronouns and subordinating conjunctions.
All of these are tricky!

1. What we desire is not what you have. 1 2 3 4

2. The car we bought stalls whenever we stop. 1 2 3 4

3. The wedding I attended when I was there

   was not what I expected. 1 2 3 4

4. You know I want what I came for. 1 2 3 4

5. Under whose authority are you taking this money? 1 2 3 4

6. From what I gather, the judge thinks

   he's guilty. 1 2 3 4

7. Say whatever comes to mind when I ask for

   your opinion. 1 2 3 4

8. What he says is wrong; I should know,

   since I was there. 1 2 3 4

WORKSHEET 85

Label and bracket all dependent clauses, relative pronouns and subordinating conjunctions.
All of these are extra-tricky!

1. If you can find what I want, I'll reward you handsomely. 1 2 3

2. Whenever we drive downtown, we see something we didn't expect. 1 2 3

3. Because you know what you do, we are asking for your advice. 1 2 3

4. I think what you did was terrible. 1 2 3

5. Flavor it with whatever spice you wish. 1 2 3

6. Barbara Knott, whom I admire for her excellent work, finished before we expected. 1 2 3

Post Test

Sentence I: Mine won't run, so may I take yours?

1. In Sentence I, what part of speech is *mine*? __________________
2. In Sentence I, what is the noun function of *yours*? __________________
3. How many clauses are in Sentence I? __________________
4. What part of speech is *so* in Sentence I? __________________
5. How many main verbs are in Sentence I? __________________

Sentence II: Is anyone home from swimming yet?

6. In Sentence II, what is the subject? __________________
7. What part of speech is *anyone* in Sentence II? __________________
8. What part of speech is *home* in Sentence II? __________________
9. Name the gerund in Sentence II. __________________
10. What word does *from swimming* modify? __________________

Sentence III: Both she and I want to vote in the election.

11. Name the conjunction(s) in Sentence III. __________________
12. In Sentence III, what is the direct object? __________________
13. How many clauses are in Sentence III? __________________
14. Name the infinitive in Sentence III? __________________
15. What does *in the election* modify? __________________

Sentence IV: Frank's brother wants the same thing I do.

16. What part of speech is *Frank's* in Sentence IV? __________________
17. What part of speech is *thing* in Sentence IV? __________________
18. How many clauses are there in Sentence IV? __________________
19. What is the relative pronoun in Sentence IV? __________________
20. In Sentence IV, what is the dependent clause? __________________

Sentence V: When you go downtown, get what you need.

21. What is the relative pronoun in Sentence V? ____________________

22. How many clauses are there in Sentence V? ____________________

23. What is the subject of the independent clause? ____________________

24. What is the subordinating conjunction in Sentence V? ____________________

25. What is the direct object of the verb *get*? ____________________

Sentence VI: Gerald, whom did you invite to visit?

26. What is the infinitive in Sentence VI? ____________________

27. What word does this infinitive modify? ____________________

28. What noun function does *whom* perform? ____________________

29. What noun function does *Gerald* perform? ____________________

30. How many clauses are there in Sentence VI? ____________________

Sentence VII: He poured himself some of the soup I made.

31. What part of speech is *himself* in Sentence VII? ____________________

32. What noun functions does *himself* perform? ____________________

33. What is the relative pronoun in Sentence VII? ____________________

34. In Sentence VII, what is the dependent clause? ____________________

35. What part of speech is this dependent clause? ____________________

Sentence VIII: What we gained is a result of our willingness to work.

36. In Sentence VIII, what part of speech is *our*? ____________________

37. What is the dependent clause in Sentence VIII? ____________________

38. What noun function does *result* perform? ____________________

39. What is the infinitive in Sentence VIII? ____________________

40. What word does the infinitive modify? ____________________